If you're looking for a delicious and satisfying vegetarian meal, pasta dishes are an excellent option. Vegetarian pasta recipes are versatile, easy to make, and can be customized to fit any taste preference. Whether you're a fan of traditional tomato sauce, pesto, or creamy Alfredo sauce, there's a vegetarian pasta dish for everyone. From hearty mushroom and spinach lasagna to lighter options like lemony spaghetti with roasted vegetables, vegetarian pasta recipes are a great way to incorporate more plant-based meals into your diet. With a wide variety of ingredients and flavors to choose from, vegetarian pasta recipes are sure to become a staple in your kitchen

Sweet Leek Carbonara

Ingredients

2 large leeks, sliced thinly
4 cloves of garlic, minced
4 sprigs of fresh thyme, leaves picked
1 knob (about 1 tablespoon) of unsalted butter
300 g dried spaghetti
50 g grated Parmesan or pecorino cheese, plus extra to serve
1 large egg

Instructions:

Start by cooking the spaghetti in a large pot of boiling, salted water according to the package instructions.

While the pasta is cooking, heat the butter in a large frying pan over medium heat. Add the sliced leeks, minced garlic, and thyme leaves, and cook until the leeks are tender and sweet, about 10-15 minutes.

In a small bowl, whisk together the egg and grated cheese until well combined.

When the pasta is done, reserve about 1 cup of the cooking water, then drain the spaghetti and add it to the frying pan with the leeks. Toss well to combine.

Remove the pan from the heat and pour in the egg and cheese mixture, stirring constantly to coat the spaghetti evenly. If the sauce seems too thick, add a little of the reserved cooking water to loosen it up.

Serve the Sweet Leek Carbonara with extra grated Parmesan or pecorino cheese on top. Enjoy!

Super Green Spaghetti

Ingredients

400g all-natural green spaghetti (made with dried spinach, zucchini, parsley, broccoli, and kale)
2 tablespoons extra-virgin olive oil
4 garlic cloves, minced
1/4 teaspoon red pepper flakes (optional)
2 cups fresh spinach leaves, packed
1/2 cup fresh parsley leaves, packed
1/4 cup fresh basil leaves, packed
1/4 cup fresh mint leaves, packed
1/4 cup pine nuts, toasted
1/2 cup grated Parmesan cheese
Salt and pepper, to taste

Instructions:

Cook the green spaghetti in a large pot of boiling salted water according to the package instructions until al dente. Reserve 1 cup of the pasta cooking water, then drain the spaghetti.

While the pasta is cooking, heat the olive oil in a large skillet over medium heat. Add the minced garlic and red pepper flakes (if using) and sauté for 1-2 minutes, until fragrant.

Add the spinach, parsley, basil, and mint to the skillet and cook, stirring occasionally, until the greens are wilted and tender, about 5 minutes.

In a blender or food processor, combine the cooked greens, toasted pine nuts, and grated Parmesan cheese. Process until the mixture forms a smooth paste.

Add the green paste to the skillet and stir until well combined. If the sauce seems too thick, add some of the reserved pasta cooking water to thin it out to your desired consistency.

Add the cooked spaghetti to the skillet and toss to coat with the sauce. Season with salt and pepper to taste.

Serve the Super Green Spaghetti hot, with additional grated Parmesan cheese and toasted pine nuts on top. Enjoy your delicious and healthy meal!

Pasta Salad

Ingredients

1 pound tri-colored spiral pasta
1 (16 ounce) bottle Italian-style salad dressing
6 tablespoons salad seasoning mix (or a mixture of dried oregano, basil, thyme, and garlic powder)
2 cups cherry tomatoes, diced
1 green bell pepper, chopped
1 red bell pepper, diced
1/2 yellow bell pepper, chopped
1 (2.25 ounce) can black olives, chopped

Instructions:

Cook the pasta according to package instructions until al dente. Drain the pasta and rinse with cold water to stop the cooking process. Drain the pasta again and set aside.

In a large bowl, whisk together the Italian-style salad dressing and salad seasoning mix.

Add the cooked pasta, cherry tomatoes, bell peppers, and black olives to the bowl with the dressing. Toss well to coat everything evenly.

Cover the bowl with plastic wrap and refrigerate for at least 1 hour to let the flavors meld together.

When ready to serve, give the pasta salad a good stir and adjust the seasoning if necessary. Add additional salad dressing if the pasta seems dry.

Serve the Pasta Salad chilled, garnished with fresh herbs or grated Parmesan cheese, if desired. Enjoy!

Spelt Spaghetti

Ingredients

2 cups spelt flour (whole grain spelt or light flour, sifted or 630)
1/2 cup warm water (plus more if needed)
2 large eggs (optional)

Instructions:

In a large mixing bowl, combine the spelt flour and a pinch of salt (if desired). Make a well in the center of the flour.

If using eggs, crack them into the well and whisk them together with a fork. If not, simply add the warm water to the well.

Use a fork or your hands to gradually mix the flour into the liquid until a shaggy dough forms. If the dough seems too dry, add more warm water a tablespoon at a time until it comes together.

Turn the dough out onto a lightly floured surface and knead it for 5-10 minutes until it becomes smooth and elastic.

Cover the dough with a damp cloth and let it rest at room temperature for at least 30 minutes.

After the dough has rested, divide it into four equal portions. Use a pasta machine or rolling pin to roll each portion of dough into thin sheets.

If using a pasta machine, gradually decrease the thickness setting until you reach your desired thickness. If rolling by hand, roll the dough as thin as possible.

Use a spaghetti cutter attachment or a sharp knife to cut the spaghetti into desired length.

Cook the spaghetti in a pot of boiling salted water for 2-4 minutes or until al dente.

Serve the Spelt Spaghetti with your favorite sauce, grated cheese, or fresh herbs. Enjoy!

Penne Arrabiata

Ingredients
6 tablespoons extra virgin olive oil, plus extra for cooking the pasta
2 medium hot chilies, finely sliced
2 garlic cloves, chopped
Handful of basil leaves
600g/1lb 5oz canned chopped tomatoes
Salt, to taste
400g/14oz fresh penne pasta
Parmesan shavings (or similar vegetarian hard cheese), to serve

Instructions:

Heat the olive oil in a large saucepan over medium heat.

Add the sliced chilies and chopped garlic to the pan and sauté for 1-2 minutes, stirring frequently, until the garlic is fragrant.

Add the canned chopped tomatoes to the pan and bring to a simmer. Cook the sauce for 10-15 minutes, stirring occasionally, until it has thickened slightly.

While the sauce is cooking, bring a large pot of salted water to a boil. Add the fresh penne pasta and cook according to package instructions until al dente.

Reserve a cup of the pasta cooking water and then drain the penne.

Add the cooked penne to the saucepan with the arrabiata sauce and toss well to coat the pasta in the sauce. If the sauce seems too thick, add a splash of the reserved pasta cooking water to loosen it up.

Season the Penne Arrabiata with salt to taste.

Serve the Penne Arrabiata in bowls, topped with fresh basil leaves and Parmesan shavings. Enjoy!

Mushroom Bolognese

Ingredients for Mushroom Bolognese:

2 onions, finely diced
4 large garlic cloves, chopped
2 large carrots, finely diced
2 sticks of celery, finely diced
400g mushrooms (any variety), finely chopped like mince
2 x 400g tins of whole plum tomatoes
Splash of balsamic vinegar
Glass of red wine
Salt and black pepper, to taste
Olive oil, for cooking
400g spaghetti or pasta of choice

Instructions:

Heat a generous amount of olive oil in a large saucepan over medium heat.

Add the onions and garlic, and sauté for 3-4 minutes until softened.

Add the carrots and celery, and sauté for another 5 minutes until the vegetables are slightly softened.

Add the finely chopped mushrooms to the pan, and cook for 10-15 minutes until the mushrooms have released their moisture and have browned.

Pour in the tinned plum tomatoes, using a wooden spoon to break up any large chunks.

Add a splash of balsamic vinegar and a glass of red wine to the pan.

Season with salt and black pepper to taste, and stir everything together.

Bring the sauce to a simmer and let it cook for about 30 minutes until it has thickened and the vegetables are tender.

While the sauce is cooking, cook the spaghetti in a large pot of salted boiling water according to the package instructions.

Once the spaghetti is cooked al dente, reserve a cup of the pasta cooking water and drain the spaghetti.

Add the spaghetti to the pan with the mushroom bolognese sauce and toss to coat the pasta with the sauce. If the sauce seems too thick, add a splash of the reserved pasta cooking water to loosen it up.

Serve the Mushroom Bolognese over the spaghetti, and enjoy!

Sage Lasagna

9 to 12 lasagna noodles (6 to 8 ounces, gluten-free if necessary)
1 ½ tablespoons chopped fresh sage, divided, plus additional leaves as desired.
Zest of 1/2 lemon (about 2 teaspoons)
⅛ teaspoon ground nutmeg.
½ cup plus 2 tablespoons milk.
16 ounces (2 cups) whole milk ricotta cheese.
¼ teaspoon kosher salt.

When it comes to healthy pasta dishes, lasagna sage is a great option. Preparing the dish starts with boiling 9 to 12 lasagna noodles - 6 to 8 ounces, gluten-free if necessary - until they are al dente. In the meantime, in a bowl combine 1 ½ tablespoons chopped fresh sage, the zest of half a lemon (about 2 teaspoons), ⅛ teaspoon ground nutmeg, ½ cup plus 2 tablespoons milk, 16 ounces (2 cups) whole milk ricotta cheese and ¼ teaspoon kosher salt. Once the noodles are cooked and drained, spread a layer of the ricotta mixture over them. Then top with additional sage leaves as desired. Cover with foil and bake in a preheated 375°F oven for 45 minutes. Enjoy your delicious healthy lasagna sage!

Lemon Pasta

Ingredients

8 oz. package pasta (any long noodle)
2 - 3 tablespoons vegan butter or olive oil.
3 garlic cloves, minced.
1/4 teaspoon red pepper flakes, or to taste.
2 - 3 lemons (about 1/4 - 1/2 cup), juice of and some zest.
1/4 cup parsley, chopped.
salt & pepper, to taste.

If you're looking for a healthy and delicious pasta dish, this vegan Lemon Pasta is the perfect recipe for you. It's quick and easy to prepare, using simple ingredients like vegan butter or olive oil, minced garlic, red pepper flakes, lemons (juice of and zest), parsley, salt & pepper.

This dish is healthy, flavorful, and sure to impress!

To begin, cook the pasta according to the package instructions. Meanwhile, heat a large skillet over medium heat. Add in vegan butter or olive oil, garlic and red pepper flakes. Cook until fragrant and the garlic has softened slightly (about 1 minute). Stir in the lemon juice and zest and cook for an additional minute.

Drain the cooked pasta and add it to the skillet. Add in parsley, salt & pepper to taste, stirring until combined. Serve the lemon pasta warm with extra red pepper flakes, if desired. Enjoy!

Creamy Tomato Pasta

Ingredients

1 pound (450g) spaghetti
1-2 tbsp olive oil
1 onion, finely chopped
4 garlic cloves, minced
500g canned tomato purée
1 tbsp tomato paste
1 tbsp tomato flakes (optional)
1 tbsp Italian herbs, or to taste
Salt and pepper, to taste
1/2 cup (120ml) unsweetened non-dairy cream, such as cashew cream or coconut cream
Fresh basil leaves, chopped, for garnish

Instructions:

Bring a large pot of salted water to a boil. Add the spaghetti and cook according to the package instructions until al dente.

While the spaghetti is cooking, heat the olive oil in a large pan over medium heat. Add the chopped onion and sauté for 3-4 minutes until softened.

Add the minced garlic to the pan and sauté for another minute until fragrant.

Pour in the canned tomato purée and tomato paste, and stir everything together.

Add the tomato flakes, Italian herbs, salt, and pepper to the pan, and stir to combine.

Let the tomato sauce simmer for about 10 minutes until it has thickened slightly.

Stir in the non-dairy cream until it is fully incorporated into the tomato sauce.

Once the spaghetti is cooked, reserve 1 cup of the pasta cooking water and drain the spaghetti.

Add the spaghetti to the pan with the tomato sauce and toss to coat the pasta with the sauce. If the sauce seems too thick, add a splash of the reserved pasta cooking water to loosen it up.

Serve the Creamy Tomato Pasta (Spaghetti al Pomodoro) hot, garnished with fresh chopped basil leaves. Enjoy!

Roasted Eggplant Pasta

Ingredients
1 large eggplant, cut into cubes.
1 small yellow onion, chopped (or half of a large onion)
1-2 Tablespoons oil.
1/2 teaspoon garlic powder.
2-3 cups tomato sauce.
1 16 oz. box of pasta noodles (see notes)
salt & black peppers.
fresh basil *optional.

This healthy roasted eggplant pasta dish is the perfect way to enjoy a cozy meal on any night of the week. Using just a few simple ingredients, this Italian-inspired dish comes together quickly and easily for an impressive dinner that's sure to please.

To begin, preheat your oven to 400 degrees Fahrenheit. Place the cubed eggplant on a baking sheet and drizzle it with oil. Sprinkle the garlic powder and salt & pepper over top, then give the eggplant cubes a good stir to evenly coat them with the seasonings. Roast in the oven for 30-35 minutes until lightly browned and tender.

Meanwhile, prepare your pasta noodles according to the package instructions. When cooked, drain and set aside.

In a large skillet or Dutch oven, heat the remaining oil over medium-high heat. Add in the chopped onion and cook for 5 minutes or until softened. Add in the tomato sauce and stir to combine. Once bubbling, reduce heat to low and simmer for 10 minutes.

Add the roasted eggplant and cooked pasta noodles to the sauce and stir to combine. Simmer everything together for 3-5 minutes, then remove from heat. Serve with a sprinkle of fresh basil, if desired. Enjoy!

Baked Rigatoni Pasta

Ingredients

1 pound rigatoni.
1 pound ground Italian sausage.
1 pound 90/10 ground beef.
1 cup diced yellow onion.
4 garlic cloves, minced.
1 (24 ounce) jar marinara sauce or homemade.
1 (24 ounce) can crushed tomatoes.
1 teaspoon kosher salt.

If you're looking for a healthy and hearty pasta dish, look no further than baked rigatoni! This delicious meal is loaded with healthy ingredients like Italian sausage, ground beef, diced onion, garlic and marinara sauce. Plus it comes together in just one pot for easy preparation. Here's how to make this tasty dish:

Begin by preheating the oven to 350°F. Then, bring a large pot of salted water to a boil and add 1 pound of rigatoni. Cook for 8-10 minutes, stirring occasionally until al dente. Drain and set aside.

In a large skillet over medium-high heat, brown the Italian sausage and ground beef until fully cooked, stirring occasionally. Add the diced yellow onion and minced garlic and sauté until softened, about 3-4 minutes.

Transfer the meat mixture to a large baking dish, then add in the marinara sauce/homemade sauce, crushed tomatoes and salt. Stir everything together. Add the drained rigatoni and stir everything together to evenly coat in the sauce.

Cover the dish with aluminum foil and bake for 20 minutes or until bubbling. Remove from oven and let cool for a few minutes before serving. Enjoy!

Spaghetti Alla Norma

Ingredients

2 aubergines (eggplants), cut into small cubes
3 cloves of garlic, minced
1/2 bunch of fresh basil (about 15g), finely chopped
1 teaspoon dried oregano
1 teaspoon dried chili flakes
Olive oil, for cooking
1 tablespoon baby capers
1 tablespoon red wine vinegar
1 x 400g can of quality plum tomatoes, crushed or pureed
320g dried wholewheat spaghetti
50g pecorino cheese, grated
Extra-virgin olive oil, for serving

Instructions:

Preheat your oven to 200°C (180°C fan)/400°F/gas 6.

Spread the cubed aubergines in a single layer on a baking tray, drizzle with olive oil and sprinkle with salt. Roast for 20-25 minutes until golden and tender.

In a large pan, heat 2-3 tablespoons of olive oil over medium heat. Add the minced garlic, dried oregano, and dried chili flakes, and cook for a minute until fragrant.

Add the baby capers and red wine vinegar to the pan and cook for another minute.

Pour in the crushed/pureed plum tomatoes and stir to combine with the garlic mixture. Bring the sauce to a simmer and let it cook for 10-15 minutes, stirring occasionally.

Cook the spaghetti according to the package instructions until al dente.

Drain the spaghetti, reserving 1/2 cup of the pasta cooking water.

Add the cooked spaghetti to the tomato sauce and toss to combine. If the sauce seems too thick, add a splash of the reserved pasta cooking water to loosen it up.

Add the roasted aubergines to the pan with the spaghetti and tomato sauce, and stir to combine.

Serve the Spaghetti alla Norma hot, topped with grated pecorino cheese and fresh chopped basil. Drizzle with extra-virgin olive oil before serving. Enjoy!

Mushroom Pasta With Parmesan

Ingredients
8 ounces* short pasta, like penne, rigatoni, or casarecce, plus saved pasta water.
16 ounces baby bella (cremini) mushrooms (or a mix of other types)
1/2 small sweet onion or yellow onion.
4 tablespoons olive oil, divided.
¾ teaspoon kosher salt, divided.
3 tablespoons salted butter, divided.

This healthy mushroom pasta with parmesan is a quick and easy meal that can be made in 30 minutes or less! To prepare this dish, begin by boiling the 8 ounces of short pasta until al dente. Reserve some of the pasta water to use later when making your sauce. While the pasta cooks, heat 2 tablespoons of olive oil in a large skillet. Add in the mushrooms and onion, and season with 1/2 teaspoon of salt. Cook until the vegetables are softened and lightly browned, about 8-10 minutes. Remove from heat and set aside.

In a separate pan, melt 2 tablespoons of butter over medium heat. Once melted, add in the remaining 2 tablespoons of olive oil, and the cooked vegetables. Give everything a good stir to combine. Continue cooking for another 5 minutes or so until the sauce is golden and bubbly. Add in the reserved pasta water, 1/4 teaspoon of kosher salt, and freshly grated parmesan cheese (to taste). Stir to combine, then add in the cooked pasta. Give everything a good stir before serving! Enjoy your healthy mushroom pasta with parmesan hot, topped with extra parmesan cheese and freshly chopped parsley if desired. Bon Appétit!

Cheesy Tortellini

Ingredients

2 cups cheese tortellini (fresh or frozen)
2 tablespoons salted butter.
2 cloves freshly minced garlic.
¼ teaspoon Italian seasoning.
¼ teaspoon salt.
freshly cracked pepper.
½ cup heavy cream.
2 tablespoons freshly grated Parmesan cheese.

Cheesy tortellini is a healthy and delicious pasta dish that can be prepared in just minutes. To make it, start by cooking the cheese tortellini according to the instructions on the package. Once cooked, set aside and melt butter in a large skillet over medium-high heat. Add garlic, Italian seasoning, salt, and pepper and sauté for 1-2 minutes until fragrant. Add the heavy cream to the skillet and bring to a simmer. Lastly, add the cooked tortellini and Parmesan cheese to the skillet and gently stir everything together until combined. Serve warm with extra Parmesan cheese on top if desired! Enjoy!

This cheesy tortellini dish is an easy yet healthy meal that the whole family will love. Make it for a weeknight dinner or a special occasion - either way, you're sure to have a winning dish on your hands! Enjoy!

Chickpea Pasta

Ingredients:

8 ounces rotini chickpea pasta
2 tablespoons olive oil
1-15 ounce can chickpeas, drained and rinsed
3 garlic cloves, minced
1/4 teaspoon red pepper flakes
1 teaspoon kosher salt
1/2 teaspoon black pepper
Juice and zest of 1 lemon

Instructions:

Cook the pasta in a large pot of salted boiling water according to package directions until al dente. Drain and set aside.

While the pasta is cooking, heat the olive oil in a large skillet over medium heat. Add the chickpeas and cook for 3-4 minutes, stirring occasionally, until lightly browned and crispy.

Add the garlic, red pepper flakes, salt, and black pepper to the skillet and cook for another 1-2 minutes, stirring frequently, until fragrant.

Add the cooked pasta to the skillet and toss with the chickpeas and seasonings. Add the lemon juice and zest and toss again until everything is well combined.

Serve the pasta hot, garnished with additional lemon zest and chopped parsley or basil, if desired.

Enjoy your delicious and healthy chickpea pasta!

Baked Feta Pasta

ingredients

2 pints (20 oz) grape tomatoes.
1/2 cup extra-virgin olive oil.
Salt and freshly ground black pepper.
7 oz. block feta cheese (sheep's milk variety), drained.
10 oz. dry pasta (bite size)
5 medium garlic cloves, peeled and halved.
8 oz. ...
1/4 tsp crushed red pepper flakes, or more to taste.

Baked Feta Pasta is an easy and healthy dish that takes only minimal time to prepare. With just a handful of simple ingredients, you can create this delicious meal. To make it, start by preheating your oven to 425 degrees Fahrenheit.

In a large bowl, combine the grape tomatoes, extra-virgin olive oil, salt and pepper. Cut the feta cheese into small cubes and add it to the bowl. Next, cook 10 oz of bite-size pasta according to package instructions until al dente. Once done, drain it and mix it with the tomato mixture in the bowl.

Add garlic cloves, 8 oz of mushrooms (sliced), and 1/4 tsp of crushed red pepper flakes, or to taste. Toss everything together and spread it in a single layer on an oven-safe dish. Bake for 25 minutes until the top is lightly golden brown.

Baked Feta Pasta is now ready to enjoy! Serve with a sprinkling of fresh herbs, extra olive oil, and a side of crusty bread. This healthy pasta dish makes for a great weeknight dinner that is sure to please the whole family. Enjoy!

Easy Pesto Pasta

INGREDIENTS

6 OUNCES SPAGHETTI, RESERVE 1/2 CUP STARCHY PASTA WATER.
1/3 TO 1/2 CUP. BASIL PESTO OR VEGAN PESTO.
EXTRA-VIRGIN OLIVE OIL, FOR DRIZZLING.
FRESH LEMON JUICE, AS DESIRED.
4 CUPS ARUGULA.
2 TABLESPOONS PINE NUTS.
PINCHES OF RED PEPPER FLAKES.
SEA SALT AND FRESHLY GROUND BLACK PEPPER.

This healthy pesto pasta dish is an easy way to put together a delicious meal in no time! To make it, start by cooking the spaghetti according to the instructions on the package. Once cooked, reserve 1/2 cup of starchy pasta water and set aside. In a large bowl, combine the basil pesto or vegan pesto with the arugula and pine nuts. Stir until everything is evenly combined, then add a splash of extra-virgin olive oil and fresh lemon juice as desired. Finally, pour in the starchy pasta water and season with red pepper flakes, sea salt, and freshly ground black pepper to taste. Serve hot! With its combination of healthy ingredients like arugula and pine nuts, this pesto pasta dish is sure to satisfy your appetite without sacrificing on flavor. Enjoy!

For a vegan-friendly version of this recipe, simply substitute the basil pesto with an equivalent amount of vegan pesto. You can also swap out the arugula for any other leafy green vegetables you have available. Feel free to experiment and make it your own! Bon appétit!

Fettuccine Alfredo

Ingredients

1 pound fettuccine noodles (use gluten-free, legume, or zucchini noodles if desired)
4 garlic cloves.
1 small head cauliflower (1 1/2 to 2 pounds), enough for 6 cups florets.
4 tablespoons olive oil.
1 cup raw unsalted cashews.
2 cups vegetable broth.
⅛ teaspoon onion powder.
1/8 + ¼ teaspoon ground black pepper.

ettuccine Alfredo is a healthy pasta dish that you can easily prepare in the comfort of your own home. To make this healthy version, start by boiling the fettuccine noodles according to package instructions. Meanwhile, mince the garlic cloves and cut the head of cauliflower into florets. Heat olive oil in a pan and add the garlic and cauliflower florets. Cook until the cauliflower is tender, stirring occasionally. In a high-speed blender, add the cashews, vegetable broth, onion powder, and black pepper and blend on high speed until smooth. Pour the sauce over the cooked fettuccine noodles and mix to combine. Serve warm and enjoy! With this healthy pasta dish, you can have a delicious meal that's sure to please. Bon Appetit!

Spaghetti Alla Putanesca

Ingredients

400 grams of spaghetti
100 grams of pitted olives
1 tablespoon salted capers
500 grams of well-ripened tomatoes or 400 grams of tomatoes in broth
2 large garlic cloves
5-6 anchovy fillets salted or in oil
1 sprig parsley
3-4 tablespoons olive oil
salt and pepper
optional: chilli pepper, fresh or dried

If you're looking for delicious recipes for kids, look no further than spaghetti alla Puttanesca. This classic Italian dish is easy to make and packed with flavour. Here's how to cook it:

Firstly, bring a large pot of salted water to a rolling boil and add the 400 grams of spaghetti. Cook until al dente, then strain and set aside.

In a large skillet over medium heat, add the 3-4 tablespoons of olive oil and two large cloves of garlic, chopped. When the garlic begins to sizzle, stir for about 30 seconds before adding anchovy fillets salted or in oil. Stir until the anchovies have dissolved into the oil.

Now you can add the pitted olives and capers, stirring for another 1-2 minutes before adding 500 grams of well-ripened tomatoes or 400 grams of tomatoes in broth. Season with salt and pepper to taste, plus chilli pepper if desired. Simmer for about 10 minutes until all the flavours have combined.

Finally, add the strained spaghetti and stir for 1-2 minutes to ensure everything is well mixed together. Serve in bowls with freshly chopped parsley as a garnish. Enjoy!

Cheesy Broccoli Pasta

Ingredients
½ cup butter.
1 onion, chopped. Fresh Onions.
1 (16 ounce) package frozen chopped broccoli.
4 (14.5 ounce) cans chicken broth.
1 (1 pound) loaf processed cheese food, cubed.
2 cups milk.
1 tablespoon garlic powder.
⅔ cup cornstarch.

This delicious cheesy broccoli pasta is a sure hit for kids and adults alike! With just a few simple steps, anyone can make this delicious dish in no time.

First, melt the butter in a large pot over medium heat. Add the chopped onion and cook until softened, about 5 minutes. Next, add the frozen chopped broccoli and chicken broth and bring to a boil. Reduce the heat, cover, and simmer for 15 minutes.

Once done, add the cubed cheese food, milk, garlic powder and cornstarch to the pot. Give it all a good stir then cover and cook for about 10 more minutes or until the sauce has thickened. Serve hot with your favorite sides!

This cheesy broccoli pasta is delicious and easy to make, making it an ideal recipe for kids. If you're looking for a delicious and nutritious dish that your whole family can enjoy, this is the perfect choice! So what are you waiting for? Try out this delicious cheesy broccoli pasta today!

Enjoy

Easy Pesto Lasagne

Ingredients

190g jar pesto
500g tub mascarpone
200g bag spinach, roughly chopped
250g frozen pea
small pack basil, leaves chopped, and a few leaves reserved to finish
small pack mint, leaves chopped
12 fresh lasagne sheets
splash of milk
85g parmesan, grated (or vegetarian alternative)
50g pine nuts
green salad, to serve (optional)

This delicious pesto lasagne is an easy way to please even the pickiest eaters! Perfect for a weeknight dinner, this recipe is simple to make and full of delicious flavors. To begin, preheat your oven to 200 degrees Celsius (400 degrees Fahrenheit).

In a large bowl, stir together the jar of pesto, the mascarpone, chopped spinach, frozen peas, chopped basil, and chopped mint. Once combined, set aside.

In a large ovenproof dish, spread a layer of the pesto mixture on the bottom. Top with 3 lasagne sheets. Spread another layer of the pesto mixture over the top and sprinkle with parmesan or vegetarian alternative. Sprinkle with pine nuts and top with 3 more lasagne sheets.

Continue layering up the dish in this way, finishing with a layer of pesto mixture and parmesan. Pour over a splash of milk and sprinkle over some extra chopped basil leaves. Bake in the preheated oven for 25 minutes, until golden and bubbling.

This delicious pesto lasagne is a great recipe for kids to try their hand at cooking – sure to be a hit with the whole family! Serve warm with a green salad, if desired. Enjoy!

Bean Mint And Chilli Pasta

INGREDIENTS
200G BROAD BEANS, PODDED.
200G PENNE OR CONCHIGLIE.
4 SPRING ONIONS, CHOPPED.
3 CLOVES GARLIC, FINELY SLICED.
1 RED CHILLI, DESEEDED AND FINELY SLICED.
1 LEMON, ZESTED.
A KNOB SALTED BUTTER.
30G PARMESAN OR PECORINO, FINELY GRATED, PLUS EXTRA TO SERVE.

This healthy pasta is a combination of broad beans, mint and chilli. Perfect for lunch or dinner, it's sure to provide your body with essential nutrients and fill you up! To prepare this healthy recipe, follow these steps:

1. Begin by podding the broad beans and cooking them in boiling water for 5 minutes. Once cooked, drain and set aside.

2. Cook the penne or conchiglie In a pan of boiling salted water according to the packet instructions.

3. Meanwhile, heat a knob of butter in a pan with the spring onions, garlic and chilli for about 5 minutes until softened and fragrant.

4. Add the cooked broad beans, lemon zest and cook for a few minutes.

5. Drain the pasta and add it to the broad bean mixture with grated parmesan or pecorino cheese, stirring until everything is well combined.

6. Serve with extra grated parmesan or pecorino cheese.

This healthy pasta is a great way to enjoy healthy and delicious food in no time! Enjoy!

Avocado Fusilli Pasta

Ingredients

350g fusilli.
2 cloves garlic, peeled.
200g baby spinach.
2 small ripe avocados, halved and stoned.
extra-virgin olive oil, for drizzling.
30g roasted cashews, chopped.
30g roasted almonds, chopped.
a small bunch coriander, chopped.

For healthy and delicious pasta, you can't go wrong with this avocado fusilli recipe! Start by bringing a large pot of salted water to the boil. Add the fusilli and cook until al dente. Meanwhile, in a large pan over medium heat, add some olive oil and garlic cloves. Saute for 5 minutes until fragrant. Add the baby spinach and cook for a few minutes until wilted. When the pasta is cooked, drain it and add to the pan with the spinach mixture. Finally, top with halved avocados, roasted cashews and almonds and chopped coriander. Drizzle with some extra-virgin olive oil for a healthy finish. Serve and enjoy! This healthy pasta dish is sure to become a favorite in your house. With its creamy avocado, crunchy nuts, and delicious flavors from the garlic, spinach and coriander, it's an easy healthy meal that everyone can enjoy. Try this avocado fusilli recipe today!

Red Pesto Pasta

Ingredients:

1 pound of pasta (penne, fusilli or any short pasta)
1 jar of red pesto sauce
1/2 cup of heavy cream (optional)
1/2 cup of grated parmesan cheese
1/4 cup of pine nuts or walnuts
2-3 roasted red peppers, peeled and seeded
2 cloves of garlic, peeled
2 tablespoons of tomato paste
1/3 cup of extra-virgin olive oil
Salt and pepper to taste

Instructions:

Cook pasta according to package instructions until al dente.
In the meantime, make the red pesto sauce by combining the roasted red peppers, garlic, pine nuts or walnuts, tomato paste, parmesan cheese, and olive oil in a food processor or blender. Blend until smooth.
Once the pasta is cooked, drain it and return it to the pot.
Pour the red pesto sauce over the pasta and stir until the pasta is coated evenly.
If you prefer a creamier sauce, add the heavy cream and stir again.
Season with salt and pepper to taste.
Serve hot with additional parmesan cheese and chopped basil as garnish.

Spinach Mascarpone Lasagne

Ingredients
400g spinach.
1 tbsp olive oil.
2 garlic cloves, crushed.
250g mascarpone.
1 tsp ground nutmeg.
100g parmesan (or vegetarian alternative), grated.
9 lasagne sheets.
100ml double cream.

This healthy spinach and mascarpone lasagne is a delicious pasta dish that's easy to prepare. Start by preheating the oven to 200C/180C fan/gas 6. Then, heat 1 tablespoon of olive oil in a large saucepan over medium heat. Add 2 crushed garlic cloves and 400g of spinach, stirring until wilted.

In a separate bowl, combine 250g of mascarpone and 1 teaspoon of ground nutmeg. Then layer the lasagne sheets in an ovenproof dish, alternating with spoonfuls of the spinach and mascarpone mixture, plus 100 millilitres of double cream. Sprinkle over 100 grams of grated parmesan or a suitable vegetarian alternative.

Bake in the oven for 25 minutes until golden and bubbling. Serve with a side salad and enjoy! You can also freeze any leftovers, making this healthy spinach and mascarpone lasagne perfect for busy weeknights. Enjoy!

Ricotta Pasta

Ingredients

12 ounces bucatini or spaghetti.
1 cup ricotta cheese.
1 tablespoon olive oil.
½ cup grated Parmesan cheese, plus more to garnish.
½ teaspoon kosher salt.
Fresh ground black pepper.
Zest of 1 lemon (plus reserve some for garnish)
¼ cup pasta water.

This healthy pasta dish combines classic Italian flavors with the deliciousness of ricotta cheese. The result is a healthy but hearty meal that you can prepare in just 30 minutes. To make ricotta pasta, start by boiling 12 ounces of bucatini or spaghetti according to package directions and reserving ¼ cup of the cooking liquid before draining. In a large skillet, heat one tablespoon of olive oil over medium-high heat. Add the cooked pasta and ¾ cup ricotta cheese and stir until it's well combined. Sprinkle with ½ teaspoon kosher salt and a few grinds of black pepper. Add the grated Parmesan cheese, lemon zest and reserved cooking liquid to the skillet and stir to incorporate. Serve with extra Parmesan cheese and lemon zest for garnish. Enjoy this healthy pasta dish as a quick, easy weeknight meal or serve it as part of a special occasion dinner. Bon Appetit!

Kale Pesto Pasta

Ingredients:

1 large bunch of Tuscan kale, ribs and stems removed
Kosher salt
12 oz. of farro pasta or whole wheat pasta
1/3 cup of raw pistachios
1/4 cup of extra-virgin olive oil
1 garlic clove
2 oz. of Parmesan cheese, finely grated, plus more for serving
1 tablespoon of unsalted butter

Instructions:

Bring a large pot of salted water to a boil. Add the kale and cook until tender, about 3-4 minutes. Drain the kale and let cool.
Cook the pasta according to package instructions until al dente.
While the pasta is cooking, make the pesto by combining the cooled kale, pistachios, olive oil, garlic, and Parmesan cheese in a food processor or blender. Blend until smooth.
Reserve about 1/2 cup of the pasta cooking water, then drain the pasta and return it to the pot.
Add the pesto to the pasta and toss until the pasta is evenly coated with the pesto. If the pasta is too dry, add some of the reserved pasta cooking water to thin out the pesto.
Add the butter to the pasta and toss until it is melted and evenly distributed.
Serve hot, garnished with additional Parmesan cheese if desired.

Spicy Eggplant Pasta

Ingredients:

2 medium eggplants, cut into 1-inch cubes
Kosher salt
3 tablespoons of olive oil, divided
1 teaspoon of freshly ground black pepper, plus more to taste
1 medium onion, chopped
2 garlic cloves, finely chopped
2 cups of chopped plum tomatoes or 1 (14-ounce) can of crushed tomatoes
1/4 cup of chopped basil, plus more for serving
12 oz. of pasta (penne, rigatoni, or any short pasta)

Instructions:

Sprinkle the eggplant cubes with kosher salt and let them sit for about 30 minutes to release excess moisture. Pat them dry with paper towels.
Heat 2 tablespoons of olive oil in a large skillet over medium-high heat. Add the eggplant cubes and black pepper, and sauté until the eggplant is browned and tender, about 10-12 minutes.
Remove the eggplant from the skillet and set it aside.
In the same skillet, heat the remaining 1 tablespoon of olive oil over medium heat. Add the onion and garlic and sauté until they are softened, about 5-7 minutes.
Add the chopped tomatoes and basil to the skillet and stir to combine. Simmer for 10-12 minutes until the sauce has thickened.
While the sauce is simmering, cook the pasta according to the package instructions until al dente.
Drain the pasta and add it to the skillet with the tomato sauce. Add the eggplant and toss until the pasta is coated in the sauce and the eggplant is evenly distributed.
Season with additional black pepper and salt if necessary.
Serve hot, garnished with additional chopped basil if desired.

Garlic Mushroom Pasta

Ingredients garlic mushroom pasta

4 ounces uncooked pasta.
3 tablespoons butter divided.
1 tablespoon olive oil.
1/2 medium onion chopped.
7 ounces cremini mushrooms sliced.
3 cloves garlic minced.
1/2 teaspoon Dijon mustard.
1/4 cup chicken broth or veg broth or white wine.

Here are the ingredients you will need to make garlic mushroom pasta:

4 ounces of uncooked pasta (spaghetti, linguine, or fettuccine work well)
3 tablespoons of butter, divided
1 tablespoon of olive oil
1/2 medium onion, chopped
7 ounces of cremini mushrooms, sliced
3 cloves of garlic, minced
1/2 teaspoon of Dijon mustard
1/4 cup of chicken broth, vegetable broth, or white wine (use your preferred option or what you have available)

Optional garnishes:

Fresh parsley, chopped
Parmesan cheese, grated

Note: You can adjust the amount of garlic, mushrooms, and broth/wine to your liking.

I want to take a moment to express my heartfelt gratitude for your recent purchase of my recipe book. As a passionate food lover, nothing makes me happier than sharing my favorite recipes with others. Your decision to invest in my book not only supports my dream, but also shows your commitment to expanding your culinary horizons.

I sincerely hope that the recipes in the book will inspire you to try new things and add some excitement to your meals.

Thank you again for your support and for being a part of this journey with me. I hope my book will bring you many happy and delicious moments in the kitchen.

www.ingramcontent.com/pod-product-compliance
Lightning Source LLC
Chambersburg PA
CBHW041151110526
44590CB00027B/4199